Rufus Is Worried
First Day of School

By Dana Kleveland

Illustrations by Elfaza Studio

This Book Belongs To:

_____

Story & Illustrations Copyright © 2024 by Dana Kleveland
ISBN 9798880439522
All rights reserved.
No portion of this book may be reproduced in any form without written permission from the publisher or author, except as permitted by U.S. copyright law.

For my shenanigans supporter, my best friend, my person and the best dog dad in the world; Brad

special thanks to Momma Jackie. We're so blessed you chose us to be Rufus's family

What if the teacher isn't nice?

What if the lessons are too hard?

my teacher is so nice! She loves me already!

I had so much fun with all my new friends. Chase is my favorite game!

The lessons are hard sometimes, but that's OK because I am smart.

Mom picked me up right on time!

My name is Rufus.
Tomorrow is my SECOND day of school and I can't wait.

THE END

Rufus Is Worried
First Day of School

Thank-you for joining me on my First Day of School!!!
It would really get my toes tippy-tappin if you'd leave a review on Amazon and let me know how you liked it!
Follow me on f & 📷 @big.berner.rufus for more adventures!
--Rufus

Made in the USA
Monee, IL
22 April 2024